Letter to a Universalist

John Punshon

About the Author

John Punshon was born in the east end of London in 1935. Evacuated to Devon for the duration of World War II, he returned home to be educated at the local grammar school and then at Brasenose College, Oxford, where he became a convinced Friend. After varied experiences as journalist, teacher and lawyer he was appointed Quaker Studies Tutor at Woodbrooke, the Quaker center in Birmingham, in 1979. Though retired from the active political arena, he has been a city councilman in his home town and twice a Parliamentary candidate for the Labor Party. He has served the Society of Friends as Preparative Meeting Clerk and as an Elder. He and his wife Veronica have a son and a daughter, both students at Friends' School, Saffron Walden.

Among his recent publications are *Alternative Christianity*, Pendle Hill Pamphlet 245, *Portrait in Grey*, a history of the Society which makes use of the most up-to-date historical data available, and *Encounter with Silence*, an exposition of silent worship in Quaker tradition in its relation to the wider stream of Christian spirituality.

This pamphlet arises out of John Punshon's conviction that to establish mutual respect and tolerance among faiths is to establish world peace. This work can only be done on the basis of what each faith in fact is, not what it can be interpreted to be according to some external standard like universalism or syncretism.

Request for permission to quote or to translate should be addressed to Pendle Hill Publications, Wallingford, Pennsylvania 19086.

Copyright © 1989 by Pendle Hill
ISBN 0-87574-285-8
Library of Congress catalog card number: 89-060789

July 1989: 3,500

Dear Friend,

I have been meaning to write to you for some time, and since so many yearly meetings are now revising their Disciplines, this seems to be the right moment. We have been members of the same meeting for many years now. Though we agree on many things both social and religious, there are occasions when we feel like strangers. I cannot minister as I feel called, because I know the words that come naturally to me are often unacceptable to you. You feel, because you have told me so, that the true line of Quaker thought and experience leads to your position and not mine.

We have never really talked about these things. Our emotions tend to get in the way, and we prefer to fall back on the principle that what we have in common is a better guide to our understanding of God than the way we state our beliefs. Yet we both know that ultimately it won't do. Attitudes do not hover in the air disconnected from suspension or support. They are based on experiences and reasons and beliefs, in other words, faith. We are both people of faith and I want to engage in an exploration of faith with you, because I have come to feel that the differences we have go beyond personal preferences and reflect a deep collective crisis of identity for the unprogrammed branch of Quakerism.

My Own Bias

I think it is fair to begin by acknowledging my own bias so you can allow for my unconscious needs when I think I am being rational. My early experiences of Christianity were all positive, coming to me through spring flowers, harvest festival, and the little country church where I grew up, with its hymns and the resonating language of the Christian faith. But in adolescence, my parents took me to the universalist church where they had attended before the war. There I learned from the minister that there were many paths to the truth.

I also attended a quite strict evangelical Anglican church to which my scout group was attached. I enjoyed the fellowship there, succumbed again to the aesthetic charm of religion and became aware of the intimate relation of politics and religion in English history. Though the vicar was a fine and dedicated man, his sermons were dire, and I developed a mild sort of spiritual schizophrenia.

The vicar's faith was on the surface, and he showed little sense of mystery, or awareness that religion operated at many different levels. But with the minister it was the opposite. Though he used Christian terms his vocabulary said one thing but meant another. He sidestepped any difficulties on the surface of a Bible passage or item of doctrine by explaining what its 'deeper meaning' was.

So here I was, simultaneously dying of thirst on the surface of religion and drowning beneath it. I had more in common with the minister than the vicar, I think because I wanted to go into politics. The social gospel was far more appealing to me than a doctrine of personal salvation. I still think structural evils can be more offensive to God than personal sins, and that is why I have always been committed to a political party, as you well know, because you belong to the same one.

You will be able to see from this some of the ways in which

I have changed over the years. Having been brought up with a more or less universalist perspective on life, I now find myself having more in common with the vicar. Is that just adolescent rebellion, or did I have compelling reasons to change? To test the matter I would like first to state what seem to me to be the strongest objections to the Christianity I have come to espouse, before coming to the matter which divides us — the adequacy of universalist ideas as a basis for Quakerism.

Objections to Christianity

The kind of Christianity I have in mind is my kind. Very broadly it involves faith in the Trinity, the incarnation, resurrection and atonement of Christ, membership of the church, the ethics of the Sermon on the Mount and the parables of the Kingdom. That is really an agenda rather than a program, because I obviously do not accept, say, the entirety of Roman Catholic teaching on these points. On the other hand, I do broadly accept the traditional Quaker theology as articulated by William Penn and Robert Barclay, notably what they have to say about the doctrine of the Trinity, and as much of it as coincides with the wider tradition. I also dissent from this tradition at some points, too, but I don't think that will affect what I say here. And I am quite willing to be saddled with things like covenant, salvation and redemption as metaphysical realities.

The first objection to this kind of Christianity is the size of the universe. Whether I contemplate images like the Ring Nebula in Lyra, or the visible beauty of the constellations on clear starlit nights, I still have the profound feeling that the scale and complexity of the reality in which I am standing lies far beyond either my grasp or my comprehension. It is similar with reflections on sub-atomic physics — as if I am suspended somehow in unreality and I could take an illimitable journey inwards or outwards and still not come to the end of things.

Now it is certain that we are the very first people ever to have access to this sort of understanding of the universe, so it follows that we are the first people ever to have been capable of this sort of response. Christian anthropomorphism as an explanation of the forces, powers and processes of the universe is naive. Its doctrine was formulated out of responses to a faulty understanding of the cosmos, so as understanding has changed it has become increasingly irrelevant to the spiritual needs of the age. Not only does our understanding change, but it becomes increasingly sophisticated and refined. Christianity is therefore simply too crude to be true.

As with cosmology, so with morals. We now have very powerful techniques to help us understand what being human involves. A range of disciplines stemming from psychology and sociology give us a convincing picture of the way our internal needs and the influences and demands of society combine to create our personalities and the pattern of our lives.

The second fundamental challenge to Christianity arises here. All it can say to the enormous scope of modern knowledge is that the most significant feature of our personalities is that we are sinners. It offers a cure for a pathological condition which most people seem not to be suffering from. So if its diagnosis is wrong, its treatment is unnecessary and it has no reason to exist.

The third, and perhaps main reason I would advance against the credibility of my own faith, is that in the twentieth century we are experiencing a subtle transformation in the way we think as well as the substance of what we think about. The historical claims Christianity makes both about its founder and the processes underlying history can no longer be taken at face value, but appear now as important reflections of the needs, and thus the structure, of the human mind. We may accept them as myths, powerful and compelling interpretations of experience, but no longer as metaphysical truths. Christianity as a system of belief belongs to the past.

Those seem to me to be the strongest contemporary arguments against Christianity; but, as you know, the fact of the matter is that I do not accept them. Later on I will explain why, but I wanted to start off by showing you that I do appreciate the degree to which my upbringing influences my religion, and that I am not an unthinking or uncritical believer who challenges your position out of uncertainty about his own. If Universalism in your terms is true, Christ is not the Savior of the world. My faith is false, and the sooner I recognize that fact the better.

An Approach to Universalism

When I talk about Universalism, I am in some difficulty. Christianity has a long past and its faults and inconsistencies are obvious. I have no wish to turn round and claim only the good bits, avoiding criticism by shifting the goalposts. The problem I face is seeing the goalposts at the other end of the field. It is necessary to have some fairly basic expression of the universalist attitude for purposes of clarification if nothing else. What follows is what I have gleaned from you, and my conversations with those who think like you, though I must say I find there is as much variety among Universalists as among Christians.

The most noticeable thing about you is hard to describe. You often use words which seem to imply that you feel you have something new which at the same time has roots deep in the past. I have no doubt that you have a deep sense of solidarity with other things and people, with what George Fox called "unity with the creation." You seem possessed more of a mood than a set of beliefs, and I suspect some of you might like to see it put that way. In your company, I am never very far from One World and New Age.

It is natural, therefore, that you should see religious divisions as superficial, somehow, and at variance with this underlying metaphysical unity. Some of you look forward to a combination of the best and richest features of the great world faiths, others see mystical experience as the great common ground among the faiths in which we encounter a religious consciousness which transcends the realm of doctrine and ritual.

The emotional pull of such ideas is very great, particularly to those who are aware of the glories of other faiths, and do not wish to be left behind by the seep of human advancement toward a nobler future. It seems generous, rational and progressive to reject the particularism of any given faith in the interests of some form of Universalism. Nevertheless, I think you need to be gently reminded sometimes that those things are not unique to you, and many of us who follow Christ or Islam have the same sentiments.

The nub of the difference between us lies here, I think. At a deep level we unite in the belief that there is an ultimate reality, however individuals conceive it, with which we can get in touch, and we live our lives on that assumption. However, at the same deep level there are differences in our attitudes towards that reality. Universalists say that it is possible to have a wider range of experiences and relationship with it than the Christian tradition could ever permit.

It is a corollary of this that Universalism necessarily stands apart from all religions, not just Christianity. You must correct me if I am wrong here, but I think its position is quite subtle and therefore open to misinterpretation. I understand Universalism to look at all the faiths of the world, from the Kachina Cult of the Hopi Indians to Theravada Buddhism, as vehicles for the expression of divine truth, and that one may find such truth in them all. But each is partial, and therefore cannot claim to be an exclusive or exhaustive account of ultimate reality. Put another way for convenience, no religion has a monopoly of truth and there is truth to be found in all religions.

At this point there is an important divergence of understanding which we need to bring out. Universalism, if it is anything like what I have suggested, necessarily leads to a different apprehension of religion from what Judeo-Christian-Islamic theists such as myself usually take it to be.

For Christians, religion is the working out in ordinary life of the belief that in Jesus Christ there is the definitive self-disclosure, or revelation, of God. For you, on the other hand, religious commitment is of a different kind, based on the continuing unfettered search for religious truth. That must be so, if the substance of religion is seen in the spiritual process rather than in content.

It is this that some believers of a more traditional kind find difficult to grasp. Your reluctance to give more than provisional answers to faith questions irritates them because they do not appreciate that your faith is not a defective variant of what they already know. It is a different kind of religion.

A Different Issue

It is here I find the conception of religion as personal process at variance with the way the world seems to me to be. There is an unavoidable interfaith dimension to many of the world's most intractable problems, many of which are to do with religious minorities living in states where there is dominant racial or religious culture of a different kind, like the Sikhs in India, the Tamils in Sri Lanka, the Turks in Germany. The conception of the Islamic Revolution as a means of liberation from imperialism has the same roots and carries immense religious implications.

Fundamentalism flourishes in such circumstances, for at times of rapid change people feel insecure or threatened and seek protection in the authoritative and the familiar. That is what we have to learn to speak to if we are serious about other faiths. Universalism seems to offer me a vision of a relationship among the faiths which is harmonious, but the situations I see calling for interfaith dialogue often involve considerable violence. I share the universalist ideal of mutual toleration and harmony, but I consider that the way to get there is by quite another route.

And that route is by taking other faiths at their own estimation of themselves, not by relativising them or compromising one's own, for example, by comparing the worst of Islam against the best in Christianity or the worst in Christianity against the best in Hinduism. When I look at the configuration of the major world faiths I am struck by many fundamental differences, and believe that in those differences we can come closest to the heart of what each faith has to say.

It is in the differences and the challenges they present that we stand the best chance of widening our own understanding, and also where we find the opportunity of overcoming the destructive narrow-mindedness about religion that we both deplore. I think that with a presumption of ultimate agreement, one knows in advance what one is looking for, and thus runs the risk of not meeting members of other faiths on their own terms.

The point about dialogue is that it takes place between individuals with living faith between whom there are also different interests. There is something to dialogue about. There is a basic faith-commitment to dialogue with. The sort of issues I have in mind (which are all part of this question of minorities) are the rapprochement between Christians and Jews after the Holocaust; the foundation of the State of Israel with its roots in Zionist ideology; the question of Muslim family law in contemporary Germany; the likely effect of the creation of a Sikh state of Khalistan on public order both in Delhi and the industrial cities of Britain, and the question looming out of the future of whether the British Muslim community should be allowed its own independent Islamic school system. These matters have a very high quota of inter-religious importance, but I do not see the relevance of universalism to their solution.

I therefore ask you to consider seriously the possibility that Universalism, in its search for common ground, is in fact unsympathetic to the true genius of each faith. The religious world is not liberal, and you cannot talk to it as if it is. The need for slow painstaking efforts to hear and listen are most needed in places like the Middle East, Sri Lanka and Northern Ireland.

I think it only possible to take a constructive part in conflict like this under two conditions. The first is to be able to speak on behalf of our faith community to those outside it with some kind of authority—which we shall be unable to do if we deny its central doctrines. The other is to interpret the faith of those outside to those within our own faith community. The same consideration then applies. The battle for tolerance takes place within orthodoxy, which stands between liberalism and fundamentalism. That is where the action is.

A Critique of Universalism

Perhaps I would not take this view unless I were also persuaded that there were certain serious logical flaws in the universalist position itself. I shall leave on one side the objection one sometimes encounters that the essence of Quakerism is to transcend theological reasoning. It is impossible to take that stance, I think, and at the same time belong to a body which exists to persuade Friends that while Christianity should remain an option for individuals, the Society itself should be open to religious seekers of all kinds, regardless of their specific commitment.

Such a position is essentially evangelism, I think. I know you are one of those people who say that the strength of Quakerism (our kind, be it said), is that it does not proselytize, but my reading of much that I see the Quaker press, from people who take the same views as you, is that this is precisely what they are doing. The whole enterprise of seeking to show that Quakerism is essentially universalistic involves persuasion by argument, and once one has become involved in that, one is bound by the rules of the game and has to accept theological scrutiny.

And the dialogue has to be theological. Religious attitudes are not logically separate from one another. Religions have structures of thought and experience which issue in theology and philosophy and provide a coherent basis for their characteristic doctrines and practices. You cannot in fairness criticize the Christian basis of Quakerism unless you also hear the Christian critique of Universalism.

My first reservation about Universalism is that, like Marxism, it assumes what it seeks to demonstrate. Marxism impugns all other political or cultural ideologies on the ground that they reflect not the truth, but the material interests of competing classes. It alone can transcend these limitations and so see other ideologies in their true light. It possesses the key to their inner meaning.

This is impossible, of course. Marxism itself expresses the sectional interests of the working class, but cannot see that this destroys its claim to stand outside class interest and discern the true course of history. So it has to exclude itself from its own analysis to retain its claims to truth.

I think Universalism is in the same position. It needs to be formulated in such a way that its truth can be demonstrated. Now as part of its working definition, Universalism denies exclusive claims to truth in every religion on the basis that while all religions can be partially true, none can be wholly so. By that token, if no religion can be wholly true, Universalism cannot be either. It gets caught in the same bind as Marxism because it cannot be formulated in relative terms.

If you then seek to argue that Universalism is a special case, or a principle controlling the understanding of all religions, you will have taken the Marxist route, using an *a priori* principle masquerading as an empirical generalization. To exclude from the start the possibility that any given religion may be able to teach the ultimate truth about God is not being open-minded.

Then, what is the universalist criterion of truth? One cannot simply assert that there is truth in all religions as if that were all. Roman Catholics believe that, as you can read in the proceedings of the Second Vatican Council. One has to be more exact. There is a difference between broad statements about truth in general, and clear and specific statements about what is true in particular.

A clearer criterion of truth is necessary at this point. Certainly there are aspects of truth in all religions, but without a working definition of what the truth is, one can hardly know what they are, I would have thought. So is there a common philosophical principle which takes Universalism beyond the level of personal preference? What is the common ideological bond which unites you?

An answer I often encounter, and I had it from my minister all those years ago, is that what reflects the truth most fully in one faith is what does not conflict with what is in any other. This is why many Quakers, because of the heritage of Rufus Jones, opt for some kind of common mystical experience which is seen to lie beneath the surface diversity of the great world religious systems.

That is perfectly legitimate, of course, but what it frequently does is to give a very different value to other people's teachings than they would give themselves. In any case, is it really true that the great world religions each claim a monopoly of the truth? In principle it is perfectly rational and possible for a faith to maintain its primacy as a guide to truth without denying that some aspects of the truth are to be found elsewhere.

Failure to realize these things has led many contemporary Friends, from the best of motives, into the fallacy which runs, "Quakerism finds truth in other religions, Universalism finds truth in other religions, therefore Quakerism is Universalism." The effect of this has been the steady growth of the body of opinion to which you belong, which goes on and draws a conclusion, saying, "Since Quakerism is a variety of Universalism we must now set about the task of interpreting it accordingly. Though there will be a place for Christ-centered Friends, Christian faith is really too restrictive a basis for membership of the Society of Friends, so we must accept all who share our values regardless of our beliefs and traditions."

This is our point of departure, it seems, you and I. There is no awareness here of the views of the pastoral, programmed, evangelical Friends — the word "Quaker" is implicitly confined to people like us. A unilateral universalist reconstruction of Quakerism can only take place by ignoring the position of the clearly non-universalist majority in the Society of Friends. You may be, but I am not ready to make this kind of break.

The impact of Universalism on the unprogrammed tradition in the last few decades has led to an almost total amnesia on the subject of Quaker doctrine, as a thoroughgoing reinterpretation of our faith has been carried out. We have even reached the stage that now large numbers of Friends think that the point of Quakerism is that it has no doctrines. Instead, the substance of Quaker belief is often summarized in a series of saws and maxims. They work like trump cards. As soon as any argument derived from collective experience is played, (i.e. from history or theology), the trick is taken by the person holding the trump.

There is no second chance of argument. The trump card always wins.

Some Saws and Maxims

The *seeker* is the ace of trumps. In order to contradict any assertion of Quaker teaching, it is sufficient to say that Quakerism began among the Seekers of seventeenth-century England, who had rejected doctrines in favour of experience and put the search for religious truth higher than the finding and preaching of it. The argument is wrong on all counts as any reading of original sources will conclusively demonstrate. That is not how Quakerism began.

Then there is the *notions* card. This says that early Quakers refused to discuss things like sin, salvation and atonement, which they dismissed as 'notions', meaningless theological terms devoid of experiential content. Hence, to be true to our tradition we have no need of theology or the Bible because these are obstacles to true religious experience. Again, the texts give no warrant whatever for this opinion. The early Quakers had a precise theology and knew the Bible backwards.

Playing the *new light* card can be tricky. It looks old, but was actually designed by London Yearly Meeting in 1931. It says, "Be open to new light from whatever quarter it may come." Originally it was supposed to reassure Friends that they had nothing to fear from modern biblical criticism, but it has acquired a life of its own. Those so inclined may now devalue the heritage of the past in favor of an open-minded attitude toward the future and claim that this is a Quaker fundamental.

The *personal testimony is all* card is part of another statement given a quite different meaning by misunderstanding. In one of his sermons, George Fox inquires whether his hearers are children of light, alluding to Ephesians 5:8. His challenging words, "What canst thou say?" (to his preaching of the gospel) are now taken to endorse the view that there can be no more than a minimum corporate commitment among Friends since the sincerity of a conviction is more important than its truth.

The bottom line of this sort of thing is that people still cling to some kind of residual faith statement in spite of themselves. The Grand Maxim of Quakerism is the claim that what unites us is the belief that there is that of God in every one. The fact that people mean widely different things by this is no drawback. It is a cast-iron answer to any claim that Quakerism can say anything more definite about religion at all.

What puzzles me is the distinction that seems to exist between the traditional Quakerism of Fox, Penn, Penington, Job Scott, John Woolman, Samuel Janney, Edward Grubb, Rufus Jones, yes, and that of the heretics Elias Hicks, John Wilbur and Joseph John Gurney. When they used words it was as part of an argument. Their utterances had a context, they were part of a terminology, they had meaning because they derived from a coherent and consistent theological framework. They used the disciplines of history and theology.

Compared with this rich dialogue growing out of experience, I find one-line summaries of a profound faith trivial and depressing. I just do not see how they can form any basis at all for the continuation of a vital religious tradition. They seem to operate as literary devices, stating and reinforcing emotion and sensibility rather than conveying a challenging and transforming religious message. They form the substance of many Friends' understanding of Quakerism, as you know, and they are often claimed as the best contemporary explanation of it that can be given. They have no specifically Christian content and have produced the situation in which, in the unprogrammed tradition, it by no means follows that if you are a Quaker, you are also a Christian.

Indeed, there are quarters where Christianity is seen as an option for Quakers as a matter of personal choice but in no sense part of the corporate testimony of our Society. Anyone seeking to say that it is, may be told (as I have been) that they might be happier elsewhere. This apparent tolerance is often the mask for an antagonism to Christianity, not an indifference to it.

You have seen the way our meeting has developed over the last few years. Many people have joined us, who, as time has gone by, have been more and more outspoken about what they will not have. Some of them have had bad trips with evangelical sects of one sort or another, others have come among us with almost no understanding of the Christianity they criticize. The nature of our meeting as a worshiping group has reached the state in which I am highly inhibited in saying anything specifically religious at all in case I tread on somebody's toes. The ministry is bland, the elders do not know where they are, the children's committee has not got a clue about what it is supposed to be doing. The one thing that is out of the question is explicit Christian teaching.

And no wonder. In place of Friend's traditional doctrines and ways of discerning guidance, many modern Quakers take the view, as I have already said, that the essence of Quakerism, and the feature which distinguishes it from the Christianity from which it has sprung, is that it has no doctrines. When any argument is put to such Friends in the form of an appeal to Quaker history or tradition as an authority for particular beliefs and practices, certain quite predictable moves tend to be made to try to nullify the force of the argument. I guarantee that if we had a discussion group about it in this meeting, each of the following points would be made within the first twenty minutes.

Look again at what I have called "the Grand Maxim." This produces the *minimalist* move which says Friends have many diverse beliefs, but unite round the conviction that there is that of God in every one. That is the spiritual sun round which they orbit. Now really. That statement is so unspecific as to be algebraic. You can read anything into it you like. As was once remarked, unless you know what you mean by "that" and what you mean by "God," it is not much help.

In addition, you have to show how things like the peace testimony and the business method relate to this "God" and that raises the question of the attributes of "God" and how you know about them — whether "God" is personal or not, or a creator or not, and the whole blessed theological agenda the move is supposed to save you from. It won't do.

You can avoid the awkwardness of this by making the *values* move. This denies all doctrinal commitment and says that in spite of wide variations of belief, Friends share many common values. What count are things like peace, justice, equality, non-violence, simple lifestyle, etc. This is, of course, perfectly true, but it is beside the point. I don't know about you, but I go to meeting to worship God, not to have values. Most of my values come from somewhere else, largely from my upbringing and education, and the number of people who have the same values as me far outnumbers the Quakers. The values argument is attractive as a substitute for Christianity, but its fatal flaw is that it explains too much. If it were true, the Society of Friends could enroll the whole readership of the Manchester *Guardian*, but if it did, it might not still be the Religious Society of Friends.

The Question of Continuing Revelation

Finally, the *individualist* move can be utilized to do away with any sense of corporate commitment whatever. It is customary to say in some quarters that the Society of Friends has never made any unalterable statements of belief. Hence, such statements as there are operate solely for purposes of information, to indicate what any given group of Quakers happens to believe at any given time.

This applies to standard personal expositions like Barclay's *Apology* or Penn's *No Cross, No Crown*. It also applies to the *Letter* to the Governor of Barbados, the Richmond *Declaration* and all yearly meeting Disciplines. It is the very fact that Disciplines are provisional which permits us to change them when we see fit.

Many people deduce from this that no gathering or body may make any authoritative statement about what Quakerism is, so no subsequent generations can be bound by any such statement. Nor can there be authoritative teaching about matters of faith which members of the Society of Friends are under a duty to accept.

I sometimes hear Universalists arguing from these principles that the Society is thereby precluded from denying membership to non-Christians, so its Disciplines should be amended accordingly, to make Christianity a permissible option but not the basis of membership. Hence, no argument about the substance of Quaker belief can be derived from the tradition because the tradition denies the authority of tradition.

Unfortunately, this argument can be stood on its head. It is a set of assumptions about the nature of the Society of Friends which is in fact open to question. Who says that statements of doctrine were understood to be provisional? Or that yearly meetings cannot make binding statements? Or that it is a principle that Friends cannot prescribe the beliefs of their members? I know you do, but on what basis?

As soon as you move beyond personal preference and say that it is what you have observed, or that this is what you were told when you came to Quakerism, you are using an argument from tradition, and are open to challenge as to whether what you were told is, or is not, a faithful interpretation of that tradition. Now it is indisputable that Friends believe in "continuing revelation." But it is highly arguable whether that doctrine will support those who reckon that it is continuing revelation that is leading Quakerism toward Universalism.

The reason lies in the intentions of those who introduced the doctrine into the tradition in the first place. They understood it to mean that we continually receive the guidance of the Holy Spirit, the mode of Christ's continuing presence with us, in both our individual and collective lives. But the gift is not automatic. There are conditions laid down for its continuance. We have to be faithful or it will be withdrawn from us. Openness to the leadings of truth in their understanding, rested on conversion to a faith in the triune God of the Christian revelation, the very thing you do not accept.

Continuous revelation is cumulative, not selective. It teaches us to believe more deeply, not more narrowly. It should create unity among us, not an association so loose that it is hard for anyone to speak on behalf of the group. It is not continuous revelation that has reduced our faith to a few saws and maxims and transformed the powerful and demanding doctrine of the Inward Light to a vague conviction that there is somehow something of God in everyone, however you understand it, if only you look hard enough.

Thus, you cannot answer the question "Who says?" by citing the doctrine of continuous revelation because it is part of the distinctively Christian doctrine of the Society of Friends and that is where you got it from. There is no continuity between your own position and the precedent you are trying to cite. You ought either to accept the tradition, or else jettison it entirely, and face the fact that it may be human preference and not divine guidance that causes Quakers to change their collective minds. But I reckon, if that is the case, we ought to trade in our Disciplines and take out Licences instead.

The Problem Stated

So I find myself wondering how all this came about. George Fox's account of his own experience is this. "And when all my hopes in them and in all men were gone, so that I had nothing outwardly to help me, then, oh then, I heard a voice which said, 'There is one, even Christ Jesus that can speak to thy condition.'" The extent of universalist opinion in the unprogrammed branch now makes it impossible for any such claim to be made as an invitation to a living reality on an official basis, and the majority Quaker tradition, which does not have this difficulty, therefore finds us very hard to understand. Why don't we go along with Fox any more? Why is it so hard to talk about Christ?

To start with, it is worth making the point that the churches of the Reformation have preserved their cohesion through statements of faith and forms of service based on prayer and the scriptures. These two things provide a constant measure of historical experience against which innovation can be judged. Succeeding waves of theological fashion and critical convention have rock instead of sand to break upon. Thus, the means exist for managing orderly change, dealing with differences of emphasis and discerning new insights that have more than temporary popularity behind them.

The unique historical circumstances which gave rise to the Society of Friends precluded the adoption of either of these vehicles for passing on the tradition. When the philosophical dualism and peculiar sense of scriptural inerrancy which characterized early Quakerism broke down, there was no compensating critical tradition within the denomination, and therefore no barrier to the wholesale adoption of all kinds of new ideas that were not Quakerly although on the surface they appeared as if they were.

Many social, philosophical and religious attitudes are echoed in the Quaker tradition. But the absence of an institutional requirement for novelty to prove itself over time has led the unprogrammed tradition to open itself to all manner of outside influences without being clear about what effect they would have on it. To welcome things that are harmonious with, similar to, or parallel with Quakerism is not at all to accept that they are the same thing.

But, imperceptibly, this is exactly what the unprogrammed tradition has done. In recent years I have seen the rapid growth of the opinion that it is this syncretism above all other things which is the defining characteristic of Quakerism, and the unique contribution it has to make to religious life. Thus, Quakerism accepts and comprehends all parallel and similar views whether or not they arise from what its own tradition says about God.

Talking to you, I am never sure whether you know this and approve of it, know it and are indifferent to it, or are forced to accept it because your own position makes it inevitable. If, as you tell me, you worship the Spirit that was in Jesus, but not Jesus, and that you follow him as the greatest moral teacher in history, but someone in no sense unique, I do not see how your position can be the foundation for the experience of a community. Your standpoint is compatible with many of these other things I am talking about, but seems incompatible with the Quaker tradition and what it says about Christ.

This is because it seems to me to rest on an axiom and not an argument. To answer the question, "What is Quakerism?" one ought to consider the whole range of Quaker life and experience in the world. One will find inconsistencies, but one will receive a theological and historical answer, i.e., a traditional one based on common experience. The other way is to pick on a characteristic at the start, and then explain the history and theology in terms of that characteristic.

Any statement of the form, "The basic principle of Quakerism is . . . " or "Quakerism is essentially universalist because . . . " seems to me to be a value judgment because there are many important features of historical and contemporary Quakerism, not just one. The argument against Universalism in your sense being a characteristic or essential feature of Quakerism is fundamentally that it is only sustainable by ignoring the evidence, i.e. that most Quakers are Evangelicals and not Universalists.

Now I look at George Fox's assertion about Christ. We have there a form of words that you do not accept without interpretation, because you will not allow an authoritative definition of what he means in terms of an objective experience. You say, and you have said to me, that Fox was certainly describing an experience, and an experience of God, but it was not an experience of the pre-existent, incarnate, risen Lord of whom the Bible speaks.

That George Fox and the early Friends believed it was, is undeniable, as I know you know. One of the symptoms of the recent changes in Quakerism is the extent of the belief that they did not. The reason why George Fox's celebrated letter to the Governor of Barbados does not appear in our Discipline is that it explains exactly where Friends stood on doctrine, and it is virtually indistinguishable from the Apostle's Creed. It cannot be denied, so it is deplored, edited out and consigned quietly to oblivion.

Now what reason can be given for denying the objectivity of George Fox's experience, or for saying that what he experienced might have been valuable for him personally, but is incapable of being an objective truth accessible to anybody else who puts themselves out to verify it? Well, going on past experience, I would expect to be told either that he was using theological notions that need to be translated into something else, or else that he meant something quite different which he lacked the means to express.

The Influence of Cultural Relativism

Both of these ways of taking Fox's statement at other than its face value depend initially on a process of interpretation. Granted that Fox said what he did, and it is unacceptable as it stands, how can we give it some acceptable kind of meaning?

One way is to argue that what Fox had to say was a permanently important insight into reality which transcended his ability to express it. He used Christian terminology because he was limited to the vocabulary and concepts of the seventeenth century, which were Christian. In modern circumstances, these insights do not need Christianity because they are much better served by Universalism. The cultural determinants of Fox's Christian Quakerism are now obsolete, so the way is clear for a new Quakerism to emerge, based on universalist principles.

Now some theory of cultural relativism underlies this, but it needs to be argued and not assumed. In its strong form, cultural relativism asserts that truth is defined not by reference to facts but to what a given culture understands. Truth is therefore culture-specific, and knowledge is a social construction, taking its place in a unified and related complex of ideas. Consequently, assertions and experiences can only be understood fully from within a culture, and it is very difficult to translate ideas from one culture to another.

This is a radical critique of rationality, yet you find such assertions begin made or taken as axiomatic across a range of disciplines nowadays. The strong form encourages people to think that it is not possible to understand earlier periods adequately, so we cannot rely on an inherited humanism. We can always judge the past by the present, but we cannot devise any standards from the past by which to judge the present.

This attitude thereby undercuts any claim to authority for the products of disciplines which take the past as their field, notably literature, theology and history. Not only is Fox's claim not authoritative, but it cannot be. The critical principles inherent in cultural relativism will not allow such a claim. It provides an excellent rationale for Universalism because it renders Christianity, and any vestiges of it in Quakerism, a matter of taste or sentimentality. You can be a cultural Quaker, but you are precluded from claiming that your beliefs are true.

Any assertion that we share a common faith with Fox and Penn is a philosophical impossibility.

Without denying for one moment that profound changes take place in human societies over time, I find the claim that we can only understand the past within narrow limits quite unacceptable. Moreover, strict cultural relativism is internally inconsistent. If all truth is culture-specific, so is cultural relativism, so what can it tell us about anything? It is contrary to common sense.

Fundamentally, I reject it because I think that beliefs have reasons as well as causes. You have not dismissed an idea because you know why somebody has it. In any case, if you take cultural relativism as a reason for discounting the authority of the past, you need to apply the same principle to the cultures of the present. So what is true of seventeenth-century English Christianity is equally true of twentieth-century Islam or Buddhism, and I do not think you would welcome that corollary at all, because your whole position is based on a denial of it.

Moreover cultural relativism raises as many questions as it solves, particularly accounting for the phenomenon of change. If Fox was bound by his time, why was not everybody else? There must have been innovators somewhere, and if they were not bound by their culture, why weren't they? Most of the societies I know about have been riven with deep disagreements about these supposedly culture-bound conceptions. For example, Universalism and pantheism were real options for Fox in the seventeenth century, and he turned them down. He was not as culture-bound as you might think.

Scientific Method and Quaker Faith

Apart from arguments derived from cultural relativism, I often hear universalist Friends turning to the philosophy of science for an intellectual underpinning of Quakerism which does not need the historical and theological timber on which it has customarily rested. What they do is to stand outside the Christian (or any other) religion by refusing to takes its claims at face value and then to apply the winnowing fan of theory to see what is acceptable and what is not.

Some Friends use the thought of Teilhard de Chardin to show ways in which the symbolic system of Christianity might be utilized to take faith (and Quakerism) beyond a Christian exclusivism. Teilhard discerned through science the development of cosmic reality toward some purpose or destination. He saw humanity evolving from the physical to the social and spiritual plane, and a process of integration and harmonization in operation throughout time.

Teilhard's ideas can be combined productively with convictions derived from Jungian explanations of human personality. If Jung's ideas are acceptable as more than conjecture or opinion, there is strong reason to argue, on purely empirical grounds, that the psychological genesis of religious feelings is found in our common humanity, so only Universalism can adequately express the facts of religious consciousness.

Underlying this is the basic attitude that the process of scientific discovery is the standard by which all claims to knowledge have to be judged. The contemporary view is that we do not build up timeless truths about the world but construct more or less accurate explanations which are provisional because they are open to constant modification as new evidence emerges. Science therefore provides us with models of reality and not immutable truths.

In addition, scientific knowledge in any given field is always qualified by its relationship to an overall paradigm of understanding in which the separate elements of knowledge cohere. Periodically, one paradigm gives way to another, better able to provide an overall coherence for knowledge, given new information.

Some Friends find it difficult to sustain traditional understanding of God in the face of these things. They find the significance of religion in its subjectivist and expressive forms which leave whole symbolic systems intact without any firm doctrinal inferences being drawn from them. Such systems, including Christianity or any variant of it, are considered empirically unverifiable. Though they are by definition unable to make truth-claims, they can be highly satisfying as personal philosophies of life. They are eminently suitable for those who desire religion but are unable to believe in God.

In general, then, I find a willingness among Friends to adopt contemporary philosophy of science as a basis for religion. Hence, the nature of doctrine must be life scientific theory — tentative and open to revision. Thus, statements about "God" are better approached as models rather than truths. Since no ultimate truth can be known by definition, religion is about commitment based on open-minded enquiry and not belief. Christianity must be abandoned because it relies on revelation, for which this world view has no place.

The advantages to Universalists of utilizing such conceptions to persuade the Society of Friends to relinquish its traditional Christian basis are obvious. What is offered here is a foundation for a theology which arises out of current secular orthodoxy and not traditional religious orthodoxy. But orthodoxy it remains, I fear. The question is, which sort of orthodoxy is preferable?

I put it this way because ultimately I do not accept any of the above position as an adequate basis for faith. They are rational, attractive, possibly true within their own proper sphere, but uncertain foundations for an adequate Quakerism. They seem to me to operate at three different levels, at each of which there is sufficient doubt to entitle me to claim that they will not perform the task required of them. I am passing no judgment about their intrinsic value, I simply do not think they can support a *theology* in the way Universalists variously claim.

At the first level, I do not think philosophical and scientific knowledge dovetail into one another the way Teilhard thought they did, and in any case, evolutionary theory has moved on since his day. Moreover, I am under the impression that this is no unanimity in the psychological community about Jung, and it is questionable whether depth psychology is empirically verifiable. You can't reckon from science to metaphysics like that, and attempts to do so are highly vulnerable to changes in scientific thinking.

At the next level there are internal philosophical questions about the process of scientific enquiry which seem to me to be equally uncertain. There is a tendency among Friends to adopt interesting ideas in this field and then use them theologically as if there were a theoretical consensus about them in the first place, and that they were therefore authoritative and immutable.

The concept of model, for example, is used in both physics and theology. But does it function in the same way in the two disciplines? Does a model work as a description? Is it a statement of fact? Can it be regarded as a principle? an axiom? a postulate? Is this the only way scientific discovery proceeds or are there others? If our only access to reality is through models, we are never likely to have direct experience of any kind. So the progress of science seems to rest on metaphysical assumptions which go beyond what it has traditionally regarded as its data and methods.

Now to transfer concepts like model and paradigm from natural science to theology seems to me to be a highly speculative business. Scientists have their differences just like theologians. Their problems and terminologies cannot simply be moved over from one discipline to another without all the qualifications and debatable matters which surround them being passed over too. At this second level, therefore, I do not think the philosophy of science will provide an adequate foundation for religion if Christianity is to be abandoned because it is considered to be outdated.

Finally, at the third level, I don't see the logical connection between adopting such ideas and a preference for Universalism against Christianity. The whole God issue is at stake here. If I were an atheist, I would greatly enjoy arguing that the idea of God is part of an outdated paradigm and pull the rug from all religions equally. I think these arguments involve Universalism and Christian theism together, and they give no reason for preferring one against the other. What they *do* do, however, is to challenge both.

I suppose, if I were honest, my reluctance to look for basic theological principles in the philosophy of science rests on the conviction that in our intellectual disciplines we find a plurality of approaches to truth, such that the humanities cannot be assimilated into the sciences. Also, it seems to me that God ordered the world so that it is not self-explanatory, and that unless we believe in other sources of truth than the human understanding, we shall find ourselves treading what history shows to be a very dangerous path.

Conclusion

So there it is. I shall not try to summarize my argument for the sake of a neat ending. I have tried to analyze what appear to me to be roots of Quaker Universalism as I have experienced it, and also to speak up for a more traditional kind of Friend. I have no doubt I shall be criticized for all sorts of academic shortcomings like bias, lack of balance and narrowness of vision, but that is okay. I expect it, probably because those faults are almost impossible to avoid.

On the other hand, please be careful who you show this letter to. Some Friends who read it might say I am being divisive, confrontational, sowing discord, etc., but that is simply shooting the messenger because you don't like the message. Actually, we are so unaccustomed to having our differences out in the open that we are a bit apprehensive about the process.

There is no reason why we should be apprehensive, of course, provided we don't let our emotions stand in the way of our judgment, or put our own desires in the place of our quest for truth. I have written to you because I know you are the one who can make the most cogent response to me, and I look forward to hearing from you.

>Your Friend,
>John
>Birmingham, England

Pendle Hill

PENDLE HILL is a residential study center and a retreat and conference center as well as the publisher of Pendle Hill books and pamphlets. It is a center for the nurture of religious life and an adult school for intensive study in those fields which help unfold the meaning of life. At Pendle Hill education is thought of in its broadest sense—the transforming of persons and society.

Pendle Hill offers a three term **residential program** from October to June. 35 to 40 persons, ranging in age from 19 to 75, enroll as students for one or more terms, joining the resident staff and families. About half the community are Friends. Among the rest a wide variety of faiths, philosophies, and cultural backgrounds is represented. Students pursue interests and concerns through study, reading, writing, meditation, dialogue, and creative projects. Each morning residents gather in **meeting for worship,** held after the manner of Friends. Pendle Hill offers five or six **courses** in the area of Quakerism, Bible, religious thought, peace and social concerns, literature and the arts, and crafts. Every student participates in the **work program,** helping with the upkeep of house and grounds and with food preparation and meal clean-up.

Admission to Pendle Hill is based upon the applicant's commitment to learning, openness to exploring religious reality, and readiness to take a responsible part in the common life of Pendle Hill. Limited **financial aid** is available for applicants unable to pay the full fees.

Pendle Hill also offers a full program of short term events through its **Extension Program:** weekend conferences and retreats; summer workshops, conferences, and retreats; a series of Monday Evening Lectures; weekly extension courses for persons not living at Pendle Hill. Persons wishing a short term experience in the resident community may also apply to be **sojourners** during most of the year.

Further details on dates and fees for all programs are available from **Pendle Hill, Wallingford, PA 19086. 215-566-4507.**

Order Form

Yes, please send me a subscription to Pendle Hill Pamphlets.

NAME _____

ADDRESS _____

CITY _____ STATE _____ ZIP _____

                              One year (6 issues) $10.00 _____
                              Two years (12 issues) 19.00 _____
                              Three years (18 issues) 27.00 _____

Please send a gift subscription to:

NAME _____

ADDRESS _____

CITY _____ STATE _____ ZIP _____

                              One year (6 issues) $10.00 _____
                              Two years (12 issues) 19.00 _____
                              Three years (18 issues) 27.00 _____

GIFT CARD FROM _____

                                                ENCLOSED $ _____